ABBA ARSENIUS THE GREAT

The Tutor of the Emperor's Sons

BISHOP MACARIUS

Translated by

St. Mary and St. Moses Abbey

S^T M^{ARY} & M^{OSES}
ABBEY PRESS

Abba Arsenius the Great: The Tutor of the Emperor's Sons
By Bishop Macarius

Translated from Arabic by St. Mary & St. Moses Abbey.

Designed & Published by:
St. Mary & St. Moses Abbey Press
101 S Vista Dr., Sandia, TX 78383
stmabbeypress.com

Contents

Abba Arsenius the Great

The Tutor of the Emperor's Sons

Introduction

Abba Arsenius the tutor of the Emperor's sons and Abba Moses the strong presented two approaches to the monastic life. For besides both being great personalities of holy Scetis, they attracted many because of the diversity of fruits in Scetis. This is perhaps due to the evident contradiction of the past of each of them [on the one hand], and their manner of life in the desert on the other. For Moses, who was a violent robber and a hater of men, from whom men in turn ran away, calling him the black devil—becomes good-natured, hospitable, a gentle-talker, covering the sins of others. And he who was called "a devil" becomes like a lion in his warfare against the devil, to the point that his spiritual father would advise him to lessen the intensity of his fight against the demons.[1] And having been a murderer, he refused to flee from the Barbarians and accepted death, bringing to mind divine justice, that all who take the sword will perish by the sword, and he became the first martyr of Scetis.[2]

As for Abba Arsenius, who lived in luxury and pleasure, living the life of kings, who was a scholar in Rome, honored in Constantinople, tutor of Emperors, living in palaces—his food becomes

---

1   See *The Paradise of the Holy Fathers* 1, A.W. Budge, trans. (London, UK: Chatto & Windus, 1907), 217. [Henceforth, PHF I, 217].

2   See *Give Me a Word: The Alphabetical Sayings of the Desert Fathers*, J. Wortley, trans. (Yonkers, NY: SVS Press, 2014), Moses 10. [Henceforth, Alphabetical Sayings, Moses 10].

dried bread and a morsel of beans, his drink a little of foul water with a great deal of tears. After being an eloquent rhetorician, he becomes the most renowned model of silence. And he, whom they could not find a better tutor than him in Rome, becomes passionate about learning from others, and with the least nod. And he, who had mastered Latin and Greek, both language and culture, seeks to learn the alphabet on the path of virtue from a simple monk. And after having for a time taken pleasure in fragrant perfumes, he is pleased that water become fetid in his cell, in the vessel in which he soaked the palm leaves, without complaining.

He who was renowned for theft became famous for generosity, and he who was renowned for knowledge became famous for silence, fleeing from men, and love for solitude. Yet [this is] to the extent that when he was ill and needed sustenance, he accepted alms, praying humbly, "I thank you, Lord, that you considered me worthy to receive alms in your name."[3] It is said of him that "when he lived in the world, his apparel was finer than that of anyone else, so, when he lived in Scetis, he wore raiment which was inferior to that of every one else."[4] While Abba Arsenius' manner of life was marked by unyielding strictness, for he did not meet visitors except within narrow boundaries and without speaking to them, and considered himself

3   Alphabetical Sayings, Arsenius 20.
4   PHF II, 36.

to have been dead for a long time so how can he receive inheritance, and censured the lady who came from afar to visit him lest she encouraged others to doing so; we find that Abba Moses was marked by leniency, for he welcomed visitors and broke the law of fasting for the sake of the law of love.

Both were awakened [to the thought] that life is nothing but a dream that vanishes away, and that nothing would profit man except the good he does, to find it before him. And although this is a logical truth, yet they put the idea into effect, and by this they moved from word of mouth to experience, from theory to practice. And consequently, Arsenius decided to abandon the palace, heading for Scetis, while Moses sought the wilderness, in hope that he would discover the true God, and as soon as he knew Him, he held onto Him.

And while Abba Moses accepted to be murdered by the hand of Barbarians, to warn that the murderer might be punished by being murdered even if he repented and completed his life in the desert; we find that Abba Arsenius, on the other hand, commands his disciples not to care for his body after his death, to the point that he asked them to drag his body with a rope to a mountain's top, that the beasts and birds of prey might find benefit from it, and by doing so, he can offer something, though paltry, through his body to other creatures.

And so, each of them offered a testimony

to Christ, and Moses attracted many robbers to repentance, and also those who were harmed by him, those who heard of his evil deeds, and those who later read the account of his life, for he became an example of violent repentance, the change of the intent and heart; while Abba Arsenius attracted many of the young men of Rome and Constantinople. This is the spiritual net, which gathered some of every kind to Christ, and they became examples and leaders.

Both had powerful impact, attracting vast numbers [of men] from Egypt, Rome, and Constantinople. It was said about Abba Arsenius: "Another seven senators emulated Abba Arsenius and practiced monasticism at Scete. Having renounced all their personal possessions, they used crude earthenware dishes."[5] As for Abba Moses, he was, and still is, one of the unsurpassed examples of repentance, and he consequently led many robbers and formidable criminals to repentance and monasticism. And in Christ Jesus both kinds lived a holy manner of life: the princes and the robbers.

It happened, in a story about their life, that someone desired to visit Abba Arsenius, to reap benefit from him, but he heard from him not a single word during his visit, while Abba Moses welcomed him, showed him great hospitality, both

5   *The Anonymous Sayings of the Desert Fathers*, Wortley J., trans. (Cambridge, UK: Cambridge University Press, 2013), N14. [Henceforth, Anonymous Sayings, N14].

speaking with him and answering his questions. The monk accompanying the visitor was perplexed. For the great saints are both doing this for the sake of the Lord, so which of the two ways is right? And the Lord hands down the lesson to us through a dream that the monk had: and behold, two boats are travelling across the sea; movement and lights and praises are in the first; the second boat is travelling in stillness and silence. And both boats reached the harbor. Abba Moses was in the first, while Abba Arsenius was in the second, both doing this for the sake of the Lord. For this reason, the lives of the fathers were called "paradise,"[6] which is full of flowers of various fragrances, colors, sizes, and composition, yet, in the end, they are all beautiful; or a paradise of fruit trees, each fruit has its taste, color, shape, nutritional value, yet all are beautiful and profitable.

His Life in the World

Arsenius was born in about AD 354 in Rome, Italy, and his father was of the great men in the palace of the Emperor. Emperor Gratian[7] recommended him to Emperor Theodosius the Great who had asked that a search be made in all of Rome—the city of

---

6   Ⲡⲓϭⲱⲙ ⲛ̄ⲛⲓⲙⲟⲛⲭⲟⲥ.

7   See *The Catholic Encyclopedia* 1, C.G. Herbermann, E.A. Pace, C.B. Pallen, T.J. Shahan, and J.J. Wynne, eds. (New York, NY: The Encyclopedia Press, INC, 1913), 754.

arts, literature, power, and sciences—for someone who may take charge of the upbringing of his children.[8] And this was common till recently, that is, bringing a private tutor to raise and discipline the sons of princes, the honorable, and the wealthy; that the children may have the tutor all for themselves, instead of the tutor directing his effort to a classroom of students, so long as they are able to afford his wages. Such scholars were accustomed to living in kings' palaces and were treated in a special manner. The students also would harbor great esteem for their tutors all their life, despite there being some who showed ingratitude [to their tutors], like Nero who killed his tutor Seneca. And perhaps this type [of work] presently exists in a simpler form in babysitters, whose role is limited to sitting with the children and taking care of them in the absence of the parents. Also a group called "governesses" was prevalent in the previous generation, whose actual work was the upbringing of children.

The choice fell on Arsenius because of his mastery of Greek and Roman literature, to raise the sons of the great Emperor. Arcadius was still six years of age, while Honorius was younger. As for Arsenius, he was raised by the hand of Rufinus, the renowned monastic historian.[9] Rufinus came to Egypt in

---

8   See *Bostan Al-Rohban* [Paradise of the Monks], Bishop Epiphanius, ed. (Cairo, Egypt: Dar Majalat Marcus, 2014), 70. [Henceforth, Arabic Paradise, 70].

9   See Fr. Matthew the Poor, *Al-Rahbana Al-Kobtiya fi Aser Al-Kidees*

approximately AD 373, with the company of the honorable Roman lady, Melania, who dedicated her life, after she became a widow, to serving the saints.[10] When Rufinus arrived at Alexandria, he immediately visited the desert, where he met a great number of its fathers, and was able to meet the ascetics who lived in the deserts and to enjoy living with them. He lived in Egypt in the period of AD 373–380, where he became a disciple of St. Didymus the Blind, and returned to write about the Egyptian fathers and its deserts. This means that Abba Arsenius had a monastic upbringing.

Abba Arsenius' status was great in the palace, for the Emperor's sons were handed over to him. The Emperor also gave him more honor than that of just being the tutor of his sons, and granted him superiority over the noblemen of his empire. Palladius said concerning him, "He rode near the Emperor. And he had executive command and numerous slaves who served him. He also did not take a woman in his house."[11]

The priest of Scetis described Arsenius' position in the palace, when some [fathers] complained about the comfort which was given to the saint in his illness, [lying] on a piece of sheepskin. He reproved one of them, saying:

Anba Macarius [Coptic Monasticism in the Era of the Saint Abba Macarius]. (Natron Valley, Egypt: St. Macarius Monastery, 2014), 305.
10   See PHF I, 157.
11   Arabic Paradise, 71. [Translated from Arabic].

Consider [the position of] Abba Arsenius when he was in the world! He was the father of kings, and a thousand slaves, girt about with gold-embroidered vests, and with chains and ornaments round their necks, and clothed in silk, stood before him; and he had the most costly couches and cushions [to lie upon].[12]

It was said that the Emperor once came to check on the progress of the teaching, and finding him standing while the sons were sitting, he objected and reversed the position, and commanded him to be firm with them.[13] And it was also said that he once punished Arcadius by spanking him for a mistake he committed, and then he held a grudge toward the saint.[14] But these words are untrue, because it is said that Emperor Arcadius sent a messenger to Abba Arsenius, wishing him to be a tutor to his son Theodosius II.[15]

He continued there [in the palace] until he was forty years of age and had received great honor, but he thought, saying, "All these will pass away, as a

---

12   PHF II, 107; cf. Alphabetical Sayings, Arsenius 36.

13   See *The Catholic Encyclopedia* 1, C.G. Herbermann, E.A. Pace, C.B. Pallen, T.J. Shahan, and J.J. Wynne, eds. (New York, NY: The Encyclopedia Press, INC, 1913), 754.

14   Ibid.

15   See H.G. Evelyn White, *The Monasteries of the Wadi 'N Natrun Part II*, W. Hauser, ed. (New York, NY: The Metropolitan Museum of Art, 1932), 123–124.

dream dissipates, that all the riches of the world, its glory, and its honor, are nothing but a dream. There is nothing stable, not prone to change, and nothing will profit a man except the good he offers,"[16] and this was in AD 394.

Leaving the World

Therefore, he renounced everything, and "when Abba Arsenius was still in the palace, he prayed to God saying: 'Lord, guide me as to how I can be saved,' and there came to him a voice saying: 'Arsenius, flee from people and you shall be saved.'"[17] "So he arose at once, abandoned everything, and went down to the sea, and finding an Alexandrian ship about to sail, he boarded it and came to Alexandria. And from there, he came to Scetis to Abba Macarius."[18]

We must always say likewise, "Lord, guide me as to how I can be saved," not [necessarily] with respect to determining the manner of life [we live]—whether monastic or otherwise—but on the level of small decisions, situations, and the service. This phrase "how I can be saved" is that which prompted many to take the counsel of the desert fathers, exerting for its sake great labor, in long journeys.

When one day the voice came to him, saying, "Arsenius, flee from people [that is, the world] and

---

16   Arabic Paradise, 71. [Translated from Arabic].
17   Alphabetical Sayings, Arsenius 1; cf. PHF II, 3.
18   Arabic Paradise, 71. [Translated from Arabic].

you shall be saved," he arose at once to flee. And, of course, "the world" has many meanings, of which are the following: the people, "For God so loved the world;"[19] the desires of the world, "Do not love the world;"[20] the present world and the coming world; the material world, the cosmos; and the manner of the world, in speaking and behaving as the children of the world. This was the turning point in his life, for the truth at which he arrived, is that this world is passing away and will vanish like a dream, that nothing will profit a man except the good he offers before his [departure]; for nothing is constant.

And this is the difference between Abba Arsenius and many others. For this truth everyone knows, but there is a difference between theorizing and application. Who of us is not convinced of the necessity of striving for salvation, and leaving sin, and abandoning bad habits; weakness, however, stands an obstacle to putting [words] into action. The person may even turn into a preacher, but is powerless because of the weakness of the will. As for Arsenius, he renounced everything.

The saint took the matter seriously. For he arose and took a ship heading for Alexandria. Then he walked for long, on foot, to arrive at Scetis, exhausted. And Abba Macarius the Great was in his last days.[21] When he arrived, he said to the fathers,

19   John 3:16.

20   1 John 2:15.

21   See Arabic Paradise, 71.

"For the sake of the Lord, make me a monk and show me the way through which I may be saved," so the fathers dealt gently with him and advised him to go back.[22]

Abba Paphnutius received him and then entrusted him to Abba John the Short to disciple him.[23] And it seems that he [St. John] was responsible for newcomers, and [at that time] it was the ninth hour [3 PM] when the brethren sat at the table. John the Short wanted to test him, so he left him standing near the door. Then Abba John, desiring to further test him, tossed a piece of bread near where he was standing, and he bowed down and ate it while kneeling.[24] So John the Short looked to the fathers and said, "He is truly fit for monasticism." At that the saint answered quietly and with humility, "[Only] after he[25] gleans monasticism from its teachers." And here contrasting how his food was and how it became should not escape us, whether with respect to the quality or the manner in which it is served. As for Abba Macarius, he prophesied, days

---

22   See *Bostan Al-Rohban Al-Mowasah, Al-joz' Al-Awal* [The Expanded Paradise of the Monks, Volume 1]. (Egypt: St. Macarius Monastery, 2006), 629. [Henceforth, Arabic Expanded Paradise I, 629].

23   See Fr. Matthew the Poor, *Al-Rahbana Al-Kobtiya fi Aser Al-Kidees Anba Macarius* [Coptic Monasticism in the Era of the Saint Abba Macarius]. (Natron Valley, Egypt: St. Macarius Monastery, 2014), 305.

24   See H.G. Evelyn White, *The Monasteries of the Wadi 'N Natrun Part II*, W. Hauser, ed. (New York, NY: The Metropolitan Museum of Art, 1932), 123–124.

25   Here Arsenius is speaking of himself in the third person.

THE TUTOR OF THE EMPEROR'S SONS

before his departure, that he would become great.[26]

His Ardent Love for Learning

While the fathers treated him with leniency in the
beginning because of his past life and his great
honor, he [himself] was a lover of learning with
humility [from anyone], regardless of who the other
person may be. The leniency of the fathers with
him is made manifest in how they admonished him
concerning the subject of beans and picking them
out. And the story, as Palladius recounted it, came
as follows:

> On some days Abba Arsenius sat with the
> brethren eating boiled beans, and as their
> custom was, they did not separate the clean
> from the worm-spoiled beans. As for him, he
> picked out the white beans from the black,
> worm-spoiled beans, and ate them. The
> abbot of the monastery did not approve of
> this and feared that the rule of the monastery
> would be spoiled. Therefore, the abbot
> chose one of the brethren and said to him,
> "For the Lord's sake, bear what I will do to
> you." The brother answered him, "I am at
> your command, Abba." He said, "Sit next to
> Arsenius and pick out the white beans and
> eat them." So the brother did according to
> the command of the abbot of the monastery

---

26   For this story, see Arabic Expanded Paradise I, 630.

who surprised him by [giving him] a bitter slap upon his cheek, and said, "How is it that you pick out the white beans to yourself and leave the black ones to your brothers?" So Arsenius made a prostration to the abbot and the brethren, and said to that brother, "My brother, this slap is not for you, but is for the cheek of Arsenius." And he added, saying, "Behold, Arsenius, the tutor of the Greek Emperor's sons, has not learned how to eat beans with the Egyptian monks of Scetis," and so he increased in understanding and in preservation of his talent.[27]

And likewise is the story of teaching him to abstain from preparing several types of food, and to not care about its variety, nor about [the way of] cooking it. The story goes as follows:

It was said that one of the brethren [living] near the cell of Abba Arsenius went one day to cut palm leaves, and the day was extremely hot. So after cutting the leaves, he returned [to his cell] and wanted to eat. But he could not swallow the dry bread, because the heat had dried up his throat. And at that time, the brethren at Scetis used to live in great austerity and exceeding asceticism. This brother took a dish containing some water and dissolved a little salt in it, and in this he

---

27   Cf. Arabic Paradise, 73. [Translated from Arabic].

moistened the bread and began eating. Then Abba Isaiah came in to visit him, but when the brother sensed Abba Isaiah's presence, he lifted the dish and concealed it under the palm leaves. Abba Isaiah was sharp-witted, extremely fervent in spirit. And he knew that Abba Arsenius used to make two kinds of food, beans and vinegar, but because of his modesty, the fathers did not want to break his heart quickly. Therefore, Abba Isaiah perceived that this was a suitable opportunity, to discipline Abba Arsenius through this brother. Therefore, he said to the brother, "What is that which you have concealed from me?" The brother said, "Forgive me, Abba, for the sake of the love of the Lord Christ. I went into the wilderness to cut palm leaves, [but] the heat greatly intensified on me, to the point that it blocked my throat. So when I came into the cell and wanted to eat, I could not swallow the bread because of the dryness of my mouth and throat. So I took water and dissolved a little salt in it and moistened the dry bread, to make it easy for me to swallow." Abba Isaiah then took the dish, went out, and placed it in front of Abba Arsenius' cell, and said to the watchman, "Ring the bell for the brethren to come and see brother Zeno eating soup." So when they came, he turned

ABBA ARSENIUS THE GREAT

to the brother and said to him in front of the brethren, "My brother, you have left your lavish living and all that you have, and have come to Scetis out of love for the Lord and for the salvation of your soul. So how do you now want to delight yourself in foods? If you want to eat soup, get you going to Egypt, for there is no lavish living in Scetis." When Abba Arsenius heard [this], he said to himself, "These words are directed to you, Arsenius." And immediately, he commanded his servant to make beans only for him, and said, "I have been disciplined with all the wisdom of the Greeks. As for the wisdom of this Egyptian concerning eating and [as for] his good discipline [or conduct], I have not attained them yet. The Scripture is true in saying, 'And Moses was learned in all the wisdom of the Egyptians.'"[28]

This Slap is for Your Cheek, Arsenius

This phrase became a maxim among the watchful [fathers] and a title for learning through allusion. It is a phrase that combines the modesty of the speaker with the sensitivity of the receiver. While a father may not desire that the reproof or warning be direct, the disciple responds [to the reproof], grateful to

28   Cf. Arabic Expanded Paradise I, 644–645. [Translated from Arabic].

the father for taking his feelings into consideration. It is a successful approach in spiritual management. For although there are people who are especially sensitive to direct reproof, there are experienced fathers in this regard, who do not hurt the disciple's feelings on the one hand, and who do not expect instant results on the other hand. It is an approach followed in the enlightenment from the pulpit, where the words are not directed at a particular person. And from here, the disciples accept the advice with ease and contentment. Nevertheless, there are people for whom forthrightness is suitable, rather than allusion; not out of pride that is in them, but because they respond [best] to the explicit, direct message. That which was perhaps [then said] concerning Abba Arsenius may be what is currently called in our heritage, "A nod is as good as a wink."

Abba Arsenius was once seen listening to a simple monk. And when they found fault with him [because] he was learned in Latin and Greek—and [by these] are not meant the languages specifically, but the culture and literature related to them—he answered and said that though he had acquired that learning, he had not yet reached the alphabet, in the path of virtue, of this simple Egyptian.[29] And this occasion may have been [related to] the discipline of eating: "I have been disciplined with all the wisdom of the Greeks. As for the wisdom of this Egyptian concerning eating and [for his] good discipline

---

29   See PHF II, 203; Alphabetical Sayings, Arsenius 6.

[or conduct], I have not attained them yet."[30] He also said to a monk who was his friend concerning Egyptian monks, "For our part we have gained nothing from the world's education, but these rustic Egyptian peasants have acquired the virtues by their own labors."[31]

This is [precisely] what we see in many people who, in front of a simple priest and righteous individuals, disregard their job, their philosophy, their wealth, their glory, and their positions, and in church they run in pursuit of prayer, persistently and humbly, to the extent that they may appear foolish for the sake of God, that Christ may make them wise! This reminds us of the story of Abba Macarius the Great with the boy who was a shepherd, how he learned from him. He narrates the story himself, saying:

> "When I was a young man, assailed by accidie in my cell, I went out into the desert, saying to myself: 'Put a question to whomsoever you meet to gain some benefit.' Coming across a lad herding oxen I said to him: 'What am I to do, boy, for I'm hungry.' 'Eat then', he told me. Again I spoke: 'I have eaten and am still hungry', to which he again replied: 'Well, eat again.' Again I said: 'I had eaten many times and am hungry again', then he

---

30   Cf. Arabic Expanded Paradise I, 644–645.

31   Alphabetical Sayings, Arsenius 5.

said to me: 'Perhaps you are a donkey, abba, because you want to be always munching.' Somewhat edified, I went my way."[32]

We likewise read about the two Alexandrian women and how their love for each other reproved Abba Macarius, and how they were on the same spiritual level as he was before God, and how he was reproved because of them.[33] And also the shoemaker, by whose thinking Abba Anthony was touched, for the shoemaker used to think that he did nothing good, but rather thought in himself that all [people] would be saved but he.[34] And likewise Abba Anthony received a lesson on exile and solitude from a simple woman who was at the river; she rebuked him, saying that he was living in a place unfit for monks.[35] And

---

32   Anonymous Sayings, N490bis. We have changed the word used in the original text to its less offensive synonym "donkey."

33   See PHF II, 150.

34   See Anonymous Sayings, N490.

35   Arabic Expanded Paradise I, 33. Translated from Arabic, the story goes as follows: "One day it happened that a beautiful woman of the Arabs [perhaps, nomads] went down to the river, with her maidservants, to wash her feet, so she lifted up her clothes, and so did her maidservants. Therefore, when Anthony saw them, he turned his gaze away from them for a time, thinking that they were to going to leave. But they began bathing. So the saint said to her, 'Woman, are you not ashamed by me, and I am a monk?" But she said to him, 'Hold your tongue, man. Are you really a monk? If you had been a monk, you would have dwelled in the inner desert, for this place is not [fitting] for monks to dwell in.' So when Anthony heard this word, he gave no answer, and he marveled exceedingly, for at that time no monk had been seen nor his name known. Therefore, he said to himself, 'This

we read how Abba Moses asked Zachariah the simple monk for a profitable word[36], and many others [did likewise]. The love of learning, undoubtedly, is a virtue connected with humility.

His Love for Stillness and Silence

He was full of wisdom, advanced in age; and we know that silence is the trait of the wise. After three years had passed, through which he persisted in asking God to help him that he may be saved, he heard a voice saying to him, "Flee, keep silence, and be still."[37] And these three words are suitable, as an approach, for all. For when you are surrounded by troubles, when you feel unsure toward something, when you need to take a critical decision, or when you are approaching a new stage [in your life], do this: "Flee, keep silence, and be still."

When the fathers perceived his ardent love for stillness, they permitted him to pursue the life of solitude. And he preserved this trait throughout his life, to the extent that the trait of silence became attached to him, for he is the one who said the renowned saying: "I often repented of having

word is not from this woman, but is the voice of the angel of the Lord, reproving me.' And at once he left that place and fled to the inner desert [i.e. Pispir], and he lived there as a solitary, for at that time there was nobody else in that place."

36   See Alphabetical Sayings, Zachariah 3; PHF II, 13.
37   Cf. Alphabetical Sayings, Arsenius 2; PHF II, 3.

spoken, never of remaining silent."[38] We read that
he trained himself for a time by way of putting a
stone in his mouth, the purpose of which was for it
to act as a reminder of the rule of silence whenever
he had the desire to speak; so he would fall silent.[39]

And we should not forget also that there were
endless debates, sometimes fierce, widespread in
Scetis at that time surrounding the teachings of
Origen, where many of the disciples of Origen were.
And perhaps in the middle of all this, the following
occurred with Abba Evagrius of Pontus:

> Once there was a meeting at The Cells about
> some matter and Abba Evagrius spoke. The
> priest said to him: "Abba Evagrius, we know
> that if you were in your homeland you would
> probably have been a bishop and the head of
> many [clergy]; but now you are living here as
> an alien." He was pricked in his conscience
> but not disturbed. Nodding his head, he
> said to him: "It is true, father; nevertheless,
> 'I have spoken once; I will add nothing the
> second time'" [Job 40:5].[40]

---

38   Alphabetical Sayings, Arsenius 40; cf. PHF II, 14.

39   See Monk Bolla of Baramous, *Arsenius Al-Kabeir* [Arsenius the
Great]. (Egypt: 1988), 32. Also see *Bustan Al-Rohban* [Paradise of the
Monks], Diocese of Beni Sweif and Bahnassa, ed. (Diocese of Beni
Sweif and Bahnassa, 1976), 54, where it is mentioned that he placed a
stone in his mouth weighing twelve dirhams for three years.

40   Alphabetical Sayings, Evagrius 7; cf. PHF II, 15.

Therefore, there was a dire need for silence. We should not, by this, marvel at his conduct; though he is a man who is able to debate and enrich dialogues, yet behold, he takes refuge in silence. Is this accounted for him as negativity? He spent his time in prayer, meditation, and the work of his hands, and consequently he found no [spare] time for talking and visiting or receiving others. And he did not usually welcome visitors, and if he were obliged to receive some of them, he would adhere to silence during the visit. This, for example, is what happened with Pope Theophilus, when Abba Arsenius said not a word to him while he was his guest, and when he asked him for a word, the saint modestly said to him not to come to visit him again.[41] And the year after, when the Patriarch was in Scetis, he sent to him [a message asking] whether it were possible to visit him; he replied with what amounted to that it would be better that he did not come.[42] And his desire to stay away from men pushed him to move to a cave that was about 32 miles [away from church] in the inner desert.[43]

The same thing happened also with the princess Hilaria of Sicily, who arrived with a recommendation [letter] from the king to the governor of Egypt, who in turn asked the Pope [concerning her]. And the Pope sent to the abbot, asking him to help her visit

41   See PHF II, 14; Alphabetical Sayings, Arsenius 7.

42   See Alphabetical Sayings, Arsenius 8.

43   See PHF II, 46; Alphabetical Sayings, Arsenius 21.

the saint. Yet he in turn apologized and sent to her a blessing, indicating that he would pray for her and that she should not trouble herself by coming. Nevertheless, she was not persuaded and went; so he rebuked her severely for her audacity, [saying] that she would turn the sea into a highway for women who would imitate her example. He then advised her to acquire what she had heard of his virtues, without seeking to meet those who possessed them. When she asked him to at least remember her in his prayers, he said to her that he would pray that God would erase her name, her memory, and her image from his mind[44]. And she fell ill when she returned and complained to the Pope who comforted and reassured her that the saint did not mean to upset her and that he would certainly pray for her, and he explained to her that the devil often warred against monks using the world and women.[45]

I perceive that there are many problems and difficulties facing the monasteries because of the presence of women, their being in contact with monks, and their frequenting monasteries. From here, many of those in charge of monasteries incline to closing them to visitors, that they may enjoy quietude. I advise you to help the monks be alone that they may devote [their time] to prayer for your sakes. And this is more profitable than conversations,

---

44 Literally: imagination.
45 See PHF II, 57–58; Alphabetical Sayings, Arsenius 28.

meetings, and letters. There is sensitivity especially toward women, because of whom the devil brings about many temptations.

It happened also that a brother came to visit Abba Arsenius, without permission. At first glance, he thought him to be his servant, so he ignored him. But when he turned out to be a visitor, the saint knelt and refused to stand up until the brother left. The story goes as follows:

> A certain father came to Abba Arsenius, and he knocked at the door, and the old man opened unto him thinking that it was his servant [who had knocked]; and when he saw who it was, he cast himself upon his face, and the father entreated him, saying, "Stand up, O father, that I may give you the salutation of peace." But Arsenius disputed with him, saying, "I will not stand up until you have departed;" and though he entreated him to do so often he would not stand up, and the father left him and departed.[46]

And of the signs of his love for stillness, the following was said concerning him:

> Abba Arsenius on one occasion went to the brethren in a certain place where there were some reeds growing, and the wind blew upon them, and they were shaken. And the old

---

46   PHF II, 6; cf. Alphabetical Sayings, Arsenius 37.

man said, "What is this rustling sound?" and they said unto him, "It is that caused by the reeds which are being shaken by the wind." And he said unto them, "Verily I say unto you, if the man who dwells in silence hears but the twittering of a sparrow, he shall not be able to acquire that repose in his heart which he seeks; how much less then can you do so with all this rustling of the reeds about you?"[47]

Also Mark, one of his disciples, once asked him, saying:

"Why do you flee from us?" And the old man said unto him, "God knows that I love you, but I cannot be both with God and with men. The thousands and ten thousands of beings who are above have one will, but men have many wills: I cannot, therefore, leave God and be with men."[48]

Nevertheless, four of his disciples lived with him—Alexander, Daniel, Zoilus, and Mark—and they were discipled unto him and transmitted his stories, though his recorded conversations with them are very scarce. And they possessed great boldness with him, despite his known sternness. They [once] reproached him for his leaving the monastery

---

47   PHF II, 4; cf. Alphabetical Sayings, Arsenius 25.

48   PHF II, 14; cf. Alphabetical Sayings, Arsenius 13.

without their knowledge, and told him that some of the fathers thought that he had left because of them. So he apologized to them and confessed that he was like Noah's dove which found no place of rest in the world and then came back to the ark.[49] It was beautiful of them to speak openly to him, while it was also beautiful of him to apologize.

Afterwards, the fathers, marveling, made inquiry concerning his silence. The elders answered, saying that had he spoken, and had men learned [of it], they would not have left him in stillness, because he is wise and full [of knowledge]. And what is marvelous is that he did not answer questions, explain the Holy Scriptures, nor did he write letters, despite his ability to write, explain, and teach. And I suppose that had he lived in our time, he would not have used a cell phone or the internet or a computer; nor would he have written letters.

He commented on this when some elders once visited him, asking him about silence and shunning meetings, and he spoke to them about those living in stillness. Then he mentioned to them the parable of the virgin, who preserves her honor so long as she is in her father's house, and vice versa. He said:

> While a maiden is in her father's house, many want to be her fiancé, but once she takes a husband, she does not please everybody. Some look down on her, others

---

49   See PHF II, 77–78; Alphabetical Sayings, Arsenius 32.

praise her; she is not held in such esteem as formerly, when she was hidden. So it is with the business of the soul: once it begins to be common knowledge it cannot command the confidence of all.[50]

With all the apparent unfriendliness and roughness in dealing with visitors, nevertheless, the following story confirms that his heart was full of love and gentleness:

On one occasion certain fathers came from Alexandria to see Abba Arsenius, and one of them was the brother of Timothy, Patriarch of Alexandria, and they were taking his nephew also. Now the old man was ill at that season, and he did not wish to spend much time with them, lest, peradventure, they should come to visit him another time and trouble him; and he was then living in Petra of Troe, and the fathers went back sorrowfully. And it happened on one occasion that the barbarians invaded the country, and then Abba Arsenius came and dwelt in the lower countries; and when those same fathers heard [of his coming] they went to see him, and he received them with gladness. Then the brother who belonged to them said unto him, "Do you not know, father, that when [these fathers] came to

---

50   Alphabetical Sayings, Arsenius 44.

you on the first occasion at Troe, you did not prolong your conversation with us?" The old man said unto him, "My son, you ate bread and drank water, in very truth, but I refused to eat bread and drink water, and I would not sit upon my legs through torturing myself, until the time when I knew from experience that you must have arrived at your homes, for I knew that for my sake you had given yourselves trouble." Thus they were pleased and gratified in their minds and they departed rejoicing.[51]

And perhaps it is for this reason that the fathers said that he overcame the demons of fornication and vainglory.[52]

The Pillar of Arsenius

In the ancient church in the monastery of Baramous, in its south-western side, he used to stand behind a pillar, so as not to be seen by anyone, nor for him to see anyone. And indeed, whoever stands behind that pillar sees no one, nor is he seen by others. He is as though saying that he goes to church to meet with God only. And it is fitting of us also, when we are in church, that we should not be preoccupied with any other matters, as one who is in the presence of God.

---

51   PHF II, 71; cf. Alphabetical Sayings, Arsenius 34. The spelling of Petra and Troe is modified for consistency.

52   See PHF II, 301.

A Monk does not Receive Inheritance

We read how he refused to accept what a relative left him in a will:

> A man of business once came to Abba Arsenius, and brought him a testament of a certain kinsman who had left him a very large inheritance, and having received the deed he wished to tear it to pieces. Then the man of business fell down at his feet, and said, "I beseech you, do not tear it up, for if you do, I shall die." And Abba Arsenius said unto him, "I died before he did, though he has only now died, but shall I live?" And he sent the man of affairs away without having taken anything.[53]

In monastic tradition, a monk does not inherit nor is he inherited, for he has died to the world, and consequently he does not accept to receive his share of inheritance from his own family. Many of the abbots of monasteries refuse to receive a monk's share of the inheritance. Also if any amount of money was found in his possession, it will not be inherited by his family, but by the church. In monastic tradition also, a monk does not receive condolences for [the death of] any of his family members; neither does he leave the monastery to receive condolences or to give condolences, because he has died to the world and the

---

53   PHF II, 256; cf. Alphabetical Sayings, Arsenius 29.

funeral prayer was prayed on him at his consecration as a monk. And this is what Abba Arsenius meant by saying, "I died before he did."

Surprisingly, while choosing voluntary poverty, the saint acts in a perplexing manner in the following stories. For it was said concerning him:

> There was a time when Abba Arsenius was ill at Scete and he did not have a thing, not even one sheet. As he did not have the wherewithal to buy one, he accepted alms from somebody, saying, "I thank you, Lord, that you considered me worthy to receive alms in your name."[54]

> They used to say that on one occasion a few early, white figs came to Scete, but because they were nothing [of importance], they did not send any to Abba Arsenius, not wishing to insult him; and when the old man heard of this, he did not come to the congregation, saying, "You have separated me from the blessed gift which God sent to the brethren because I was unworthy to partake of it." And when the old men heard [this], they profited [greatly] by his humility, and the priest went and carried some of the figs to him, and brought him to the congregation with great joy.[55]

---

54 Alphabetical Sayings, Arsenius 20; cf. PHF II, 35.
55 PHF II, 109; cf. Alphabetical Sayings, Arsenius 16.

From these two stories, we are assured that while the saint refuses to take a huge amount of money which is considered legally his own, he humbly receives alms, without getting low self-esteem. He also affirms that he is a member of the body of the monastery, and that he is not ashamed to divide a morsel of food with his brothers.

His Spiritual Struggles

The most important thing that we need to examine in the lives of the saints is their manner of life and their spiritual conduct. As for miracles, they are a proof of their holiness, and the honor God has for them. It was said of the saint that no one was able to realize and attain to the knowledge of his conduct and struggle.[56] And all that his disciples recorded is that he would work for six hours in the day[57] and would spend the remaining time and the whole night in prayer.[58] And if he had to sleep a little, he would say to sleep[59], "Come on, you wicked slave."[60] The fathers were very sensitive with respect to sleep, to the extent that they exchanged the word "sleep" with "rest." The saint sees that one hour of sleep per day is sufficient for a monk. While many people see that a person must sleep for eight hours per day, some

56   See PHF II, 24; Alphabetical Sayings, Arsenius S1.
57   See PHF II, 46; Alphabetical Sayings, Arsenius 18.
58   See PHF II, 30; Alphabetical Sayings, Arsenius 14.
59   Arabic text: himself.
60   See PHF II, 30; Alphabetical Sayings, Arsenius 14.

specialists and those who have experience assert that the body, through habit, may be satisfied with less than that, without any effect on the productivity of the person, just like the stomach which gets used to being small or large in size.

The saint used to frequently keep vigils in prayer and praising. For the following was said of him:

> He used to spend the whole night watching and toward dawn, when naturally he wanted to sleep, he would say to sleep: "Come on then, wicked slave," and he would snatch a little, sitting down, then get up straight away.[61]

And he used to say, "One hour's sleep is sufficient for a monk, provided that he be strenuous."[62]

He was not accustomed to changing the water with which he soaked the palm leaves, but he would add water to it [when the water was diminished in the vessel], so that it reeked. And when Abba Macarius the Alexandrian visited him and noticed that, Abba Arsenius answered him that though he cannot stand it, he bears it in place of all the sweet aromas in which he delighted in the world.[63] He also used to place a rag on his lap, while he plaited, to

---

61   Alphabetical Sayings, Arsenius 14.

62   PHF II, 30; cf. Alphabetical Sayings, Arsenius 15.

63   See PHF II, 46; Alphabetical Sayings, Arsenius 18; Arabic Paradise, 75.

wipe his tears with, but his tears would even soak the palm leaves.[64] And concerning tears, which carved grooves on the sides of his nose,[65] they were not the tears of sorrow or despair, but the tears of sweet consolation, which, cleansing, give rest.

When Abba Poemen heard of his repose, he said:

Blessed are you, O Abba Arsenius, for you wept over yourself in this world. For he who does not weep for himself in this world must weep for ever in the next. He may weep here voluntarily, or there because of the punishments [which he will receive], but it is impossible for a man to escape weeping either here or there.[66]

And despite his arduous struggle and his much toil with respect to self-restraint toward food, drink, sleep, money, and the matters of the world, and also the positive struggle in prayer and praising, he considered himself weak, not having begun the monastic path yet! The following was recounted about him:

On one occasion when Abba Arsenius was in his cell the devils rose up against him and vexed him; and those who used to minister to him came to him, and as they stood

---

64   See Alphabetical Sayings, Arsenius 41; Arabic Paradise, 75.

65   Arabic Expanded Paradise I, 659.

66   PHF II, 34; cf. Alphabetical Sayings, Arsenius 41.

outside his cell they heard him crying out to God, saying, "O God, do not forsake me. I have never done before You anything which is good, but grant, O Lord, according to Your grace, that I may begin in the way."[67]

His Movements

He lived in solitude for forty years at a distance of 32 miles from the church (the center of Scetis), and therefore he did not leave the desert after the first raid of the Barbarians in AD 407. At the end of forty year, the second raid took place in AD 434, so he left Scetis, weeping, and said his famous saying, "The world has lost Rome, the Monks Scete."[68]

He went to Troe and dwelt for ten years in Shahran monastery in Mount Mokattam (Al Maadi now), and at the end of the ten years, he left for Alexandria, where he dwelt for three years in Canopus, beside Abu Qir.[69] After that he returned to Troe in AD 447. And there is currently a church after his name in the Diocese of Al Maadi. And it is mentioned that when his disciples reproved him for leaving them without a reason, he answered, saying, "The dove could not find rest for the sole of her

---

67 PHF II, 123; cf. Alphabetical Sayings, Arsenius 3.

68 Alphabetical Sayings, Arsenius 21.

69 See PHF II, 36; Alphabetical Sayings, Arsenius 42.

foot, and she returned to Noah in the ark."[70] And they were pleased with this amiable apology, as we have previously said.

His Final Days and Departure

The saint spent his final two years ill in Troe.[71] When his departure drew near, he called his disciples and informed them of it, and they asked him naively what they should do with his body. He said to them, "Do not disturb yourselves by weeping for me. Look, I am standing with you before the fearful seat of judgment of Christ, so when my hour comes, do not give my body to anyone."[72] They said to him, "What then do we do, for we do not know how to shroud it [for burial]?" The elder said to them, "Do you not know how to tie rope around my foot and drag me to the mountain for the benefit of the beasts and birds of prey?"[73]

We marvel at how he lived in the shadow, hidden throughout his monastic life, yet at his death, he asked that his body be exposed, to be food for beasts; all the while, many fathers, both in ancient and recent times, command that their bodies and bones should be well taken care of, where they should be buried, and how they should be taken

---

70 PHF II, 123; cf. Alphabetical Sayings, Arsenius 32.

71 See PHF II, 36; Alphabetical Sayings, Arsenius 42.

72 See PHF II, 123; Alphabetical Sayings, Arsenius 40.

73 Ibid.

care of. And there are some who make fascinating tombs for themselves, spending a fortune on them, and command that they should be guarded and taken care of.

Here I would like to admonish those who care about appearances in funerals, the number of people in attendance, the appearance of the obituary and its content, the coffin and its cost, the number of the letters of condolence that were received, the number of priests attending the farewell, who wrote about the departed, and other such matters. And they forget that which is more important—that is, the future of the departed themselves and their eternal fate.

When the time of his death drew near, he called his disciples, consoled them, and exhorted them, saying to them, "Know that my time has drawn near; therefore, care about nothing except the salvation of your souls."[74]

When the blessed Arsenius was about to deliver his spirit the brethren saw him weeping, and they said unto him, "Are you also afraid, O father?" And he said unto them, "The dread of this hour has been with me in very truth from the time when I became a monk, and was afraid." And so he died.[75]

---

74   Arabic Paradise, 84.

75   PHF II, 34; cf. Alphabetical Sayings, Arsenius 40.

"And his tears flowed out from his eyes.... So his disciples wept bitterly, kissed his feet, and bid him farewell, like a foreigner who desired to travel to his true country."[76] He left our world on Pashons 13 (May 21), AD 449. So his disciples took his body and buried it in the monastery's burial place, and a church and a monastery were built over it by the hand of the Roman king.[77] His disciple Daniel said that he had left him his leather coat, his white shirt, and his palm-leaf sandals, and that he used to put them on for a blessing.[78]

When Pope Theophilus heard of his death, he said, "Blessed are you, O Abba Arsenius, because for this hour you wept all the days of your life."[79]

After his departure, his disciple commented, saying:

> Now his face was like that of an angel, and his hair was as white as snow, and as abundant as that of Jacob. [He was perfect in his old age, healthy in body, smiling][80]. His body was dry by reason of his labors, and his beard descended to his belly, but

---

76   Arabic Paradise, 84.

77   See Fr. Matthew the Poor, A*l-Rahbana Al-Kobtiya fi Aser Al-Kidees Anba Macarius* [Coptic Monasticism in the Era of the Saint Abba Macarius]. (Natron Valley, Egypt: St. Macarius Monastery, 2014), 309.

78   See Alphabetical Sayings, Arsenius 42.

79   Arabic Paradise, 85. [Translated from Arabic]. Cf. PHF II, 33; Alphabetical Sayings, Theophilus 5.

80   This statement appears in the Arabic Paradise, 85.

his eyelashes were destroyed by weeping; he was tall in stature, but somewhat bowed by old age and he ended his days when he was ninety-five years old. He lived in the world, in the palace, for forty years, in the days of Theodosius, the great king, who became the father of the Emperors Honorius and Arcadius, and he lived in Scetis forty years, and he lived for ten years in Troe of Babylon which is opposite the Memphis which is in Egypt, and he dwelt for three years in Canopus of Alexandria, and during the two remaining years he came to Troe again, where he died. And he finished his career in peace and in the fear of God.[81]

And his disciple continues, saying:

For he was a good man, full of the Holy Spirit and of faith" [Acts 11:24]. "He left me his leather tunic, his shirt of white wool, and his palm-leaf sandals and, unworthy though I be, I wore them to receive a blessing.[82]

Some of the Teachings of Abba Arsenius

Abba Arsenius said to his disciples before his departure, "Three things are of the goodness

---

81 PHF II, 36–37; cf. Alphabetical Sayings, Arsenius 42.

82 Alphabetical Sayings, Arsenius 42.

of the mind: faith in God, patience in every ordeal, and toil of the body that it may be humbled.

"Three matters the mind rejoices in: discernment of good from evil, thinking of a matter before doing it, and staying away from guile.

"Three things the mind is enlightened with: doing good to those who wrong you, enduring what befalls you from your enemies, and abandoning looking at and envying those who are ahead of you in the world.

"Six things the mind is purified with: silence, keeping the commandments, abstinence from food, trust in God in all matters along with giving up the reliance on any ruler of the world, suppressing the heart from thinking evil, refraining from listening to the words of the wealthy, refraining from looking at women.

"Four [things] preserve the soul: [showing] mercy to all men, abandoning anger, endurance, and removing the guilt and casting it out of your heart through praising.

"Four [things] preserve a young man from a bad thought: reading the books of the commandments, casting out laziness, rising up at night for prayer and supplication, and always being humble.

"Three [things] darken the soul: walking in cities and towns, looking at the glory of the world, and mingling with the rulers in the world.

"From four things the defilement of the body arises: taking one's fill of food, overindulgence in drinking, much sleeping, and cleaning the body with water and perfume, and caring about this at all times.

"Four [things] blind the soul: hatred toward your brother, especially contempt for the poor, envy, and backbiting.

"Four [things] cause the perdition of the soul and its loss: wandering from one place to another, the love of meeting the people of the world, excessive luxury and extravagance, the abundance of rancor in the heart.

"Four [things] lead to anger: dealings, bargaining, adamance on your opinion regarding the desire of your soul, and overruling others' counsel while following your own desires.

"Three [things] if a person does, he dwells in the kingdom: unceasing grief and sighing, weeping for sins and iniquities, awaiting death every day and hour.

"Three [things] war against the mind: forgetfulness, laziness, and the abandonment of prayer."[83]

✤✤✤

A brother asked Abba Arsenius if he could hear a saying from him. The elder said to him: "As much as you are able, strive so that what goes on inside you be godly and you conquer your external passions."[84]

✤✤✤

A certain brother came to Abba Arsenius, and said unto him, "My thoughts vex me, and say, 'You cannot fast; and you are not able to labor, therefore visit the sick, which is a great commandment.'" Then Abba Arsenius, after the manner of one who was well acquainted with the war of devils, said unto him, "Eat, drink, and sleep, and toil not, but on no account go out of your cell." For the old man knew that dwelling constantly in the cell induces all the habits of the solitary life. And when the brother

---

83   Arabic Paradise, 83–84. [Translated from Arabic]. Also cf. Isaiah of Scetis, *Ascetic Discourses,* J. Chryssavgis and P. Penkett, trans. (Kalamazoo, Michigan: Cistercian Publications, 2002), 81–82.

84   Alphabetical Sayings, Arsenius 9.

had done these things for three days, he became weary of idleness, and finding a few palm leaves on the ground, he took them and began to split them up, and on the following day he dipped them in water and began to work (i.e. to weave baskets); and when he felt hungry he said, "I will finish one more small piece of work, and then I will eat." And when he was reading in the Book, he said, "I will sing a few Psalms and say a few prayers, and then I will eat without any compunction[85]." Thus little by little, by the agency of God, he advanced in the ascetic life until he reached the first rank, and received the power to resist the thoughts and to vanquish them.[86]

✛✛✛

Another asked him:

"Why am I afflicted by accidie when I am staying in my cell?" "Because you have not yet seen either the repose for which one hopes or the punishment which lies ahead," he replied. "If you had really seen them, even if your cell were filled with worms so that

---

85   "Compunction" appears as "concern" in the Alphabetical and Anonymous Sayings.

86   PHF II, 4–5; cf. Alphabetical Sayings, Arsenius 11; cf. Anonymous Sayings, N195.

you feared [they would be] right up to your neck, you would patiently endure without falling into accidie."[87]

---

87   Anonymous Sayings, N196. In Arabic, this saying is attributed to Abba Arsenius.

www.ingramcontent.com/pod-product-compliance
Lightning Source LLC
Chambersburg PA
CBHW021118020426
42331CB00004B/537